Jams&
Preserves

igloobooks
.com

Published in 2012
by Igloo Books Ltd
Cottage Farm
Sywell
NN6 0BJ
www.igloobooks.com

Food photography and recipe development: PhotoCuisine UK
Front and back cover images © PhotoCuisine UK

H005 0812
2 4 6 8 10 9 7 5 3 1
ISBN 978-0-85780-730-4

Printed and manufactured in China

Jams&
Preserves

Contents

Jams

Apricot Jam

INGREDIENTS

1 kg / 2 lb 4 oz / 5 cups fresh apricots,
de-stoned and roughly chopped
700 g / 1 lb 9 oz / 3 cups granulated sugar
110 g / 4 oz / ½ cup ground almonds
30 g / 1 oz / 2 tbsp flaked (slivered)
almonds

METHOD

Combine the apricot and sugar in a large mixing bowl.

Toss well and cover with a tea towel before leaving overnight.

The next day, place a couple of saucers in the freezer; they will be needed for testing the jam's setting point.

Preheat the oven to 170°C (150° fan) / 325F / gas 3.

Place the jars in the oven to sterilise with their lids.

Place the fruit and sugar mixture in a large stainless steel saucepan and cook over a high heat for 15 minutes, stirring occasionally.

Remove the saucepan from the heat and spoon a teaspoon of the hot jam onto the cold saucers from the freezer; when the jam has cooled, prod it to see if a skin has formed. If it has, the jam is ready. If not, continue boiling for a few more minutes before testing again.

Once the jam is set, add the butter and almonds and stir well until the butter has dissolved into the jam.

Spoon the hot jam into the jars.

Cover the tops with a waxed disc before sealing well.

Let the jam cool to room temperature before serving with a sprinkle of flaked almonds on top.

Makes: two 500 g jars | Preparation time : 15-20 minutes | Cooking time : 25-30 minutes

Pineapple Jam

INGREDIENTS

500 g / 1 lb 2 oz / 2 cups pineapple chunks, drained
500 g / 1 lb 2 oz / 2 ¼ cups caster (superfine) sugar
1.25 l / 2 pints 4 fl. oz / 5 cups cold water
1 tsp citric acid

METHOD

Place a couple of saucers in the freezer for testing purposes.

Combine the pineapple and water in a large stainless steel saucepan.

Cook over a medium heat, stirring frequently, until there is about 500 ml of water left.

Add the sugar and continue to cook over a slightly reduced heat, stirring occasionally, until the sugar has dissolved.

Once the sugar has dissolved, add the citric acid and boil for 6-8 minutes.

Preheat the oven to 170°C (150° fan) / 325F / gas 3.

Place the jars in the oven for 10 minutes, with their lids to sterilise.

Remove the saucepan from the heat and spoon a teaspoon of the hot jam onto the cold saucers from the freezer; when the jam has cooled, prod it to see if a skin has formed. If it has, the jam is ready. If not, continue boiling for a few more minutes before testing again.

Once the jam is ready to set, remove it from the heat.

Remove the jars and their lids from the oven and spoon the hot jam into them.

Cover the tops with waxed discs before sealing well.

Let the jam cool to room temperature before serving or storing.

Makes: two 500 g jars | Preparation time : 10 minutes | Cooking time : 35-40 minutes

Purple Fig Jam

INGREDIENTS

450 g / 1 lb / 3 cups purple figs, quartered
225 g / 8 oz / 1 cup caster (superfine) sugar
225 g / 8 oz / 1 cup honey
250 ml / 9 fl. oz / 1 cup water
2 tsp butter

METHOD

Preheat the oven to 170°C (150° fan) / 325F / gas 3.

Place a couple of saucers in the freezer; they will be needed for testing the jam's setting point.

Combine the figs and water in a large saucepan and cook over a medium heat, stirring occasionally, until the fruit softens.

Once soft, add the sugar and honey and stir well, scraping down the sides of the saucepan.

Reduce the heat and simmer the fruit, sugar and honey for 10-15 minutes until the sugar has dissolved, stirring the jam occasionally.

Once the sugar has dissolved, increase the heat and boil the jam for 10 minutes.

Remove the saucepan from the heat and spoon a teaspoon of the hot jam onto the cold saucers from the freezer; when the jam has cooled, prod it to see if a skin has formed. If it has, the jam is ready. If not, continue boiling for a few more minutes before testing again.

Once the jam is ready to set, add the butter and stir well until dissolved into the jam.

Place the jar in the oven with its lid to sterilise it.

Remove after 10 minutes and place on a flat, heatproof surface.

Spoon the jam into the jar and cover the top with a waxed disc.

Seal well and let the jar cool to room temperature before serving.

Makes: one 500 g jar | Preparation time : 10 minutes | Cooking time : 30-35 minutes

Rhubarb and Orange Jam

INGREDIENTS

2 sticks rhubarb, peeled and diced
4 oranges, juiced
2 oranges, peel and skin removed,
then diced
450 g / 1 lb / 2 cups granulated sugar
750 ml / 1 pint 7 fl. oz / 3 cups cold water
6 leaves gelatine

METHOD

Combine the orange juice, water and sugar in a large, stainless
steel saucepan.

Heat over a medium heat until the sugar has dissolved, then add
the rhubarb and diced orange and simmer the fruit for 10-12 minutes
over a reduced heat until soft.

Soften the gelatine leaves in a little cold water and leave for 10 minutes.

Remove the orange and rhubarb fruit syrup from the heat, then squeeze
out the excess water from the gelatine leaves and add to the hot syrup,
whisking gently until dissolved.

Set the saucepan to one side and preheat the oven to 170°C
(150° fan) / 325F / gas 3.

Place the jars with their lids in the oven to sterilise.

Leave them for 10 minutes then remove from the oven.

Divide the fruit and the hot syrup between the jars and seal well.

Let them cool to room temperature before chilling overnight until set.

Makes: two 500 g jars | Preparation time : 15 minutes | Cooking time : 25-30 minutes

Peach and Raisin Jam

INGREDIENTS

4 large peaches, de-stoned and diced
110 g / 4 oz / ½ cup caster (superfine)
sugar
100 ml / 3 ½ fl. oz / ⅓ cup distilled
white vinegar
100 g / 3 ½ oz / ½ cup raisins
1 tsp whole cloves
1 stick cinnamon
¼ tsp ground cloves
¼ tsp ground cinnamon

METHOD

Combine the vinegar, sugar, whole and ground spices in a large saucepan set over a medium heat and cook until the sugar has dissolved and you have a thin syrup.

Add the peach and stir well.

Cook the mixture at a gentle simmer for 40-45 minutes, stirring occasionally, until you have a thick jam.

Preheat the oven to 170°C (150° fan) / 325F / gas 3.

Place the jar in the oven with its lid to sterilise.

Remove after 10 minutes and place on a flat, heatproof surface.

Spoon the jam into the jar, discarding the cinnamon stick as you do and cover the top with a waxed disc.

Seal well and let the jam cool to room temperature before serving.

Makes: one 500 g jar | Preparation time : 15 minutes | Cooking time : 45-50 minutes

Four Fruit Jam

INGREDIENTS

250 g / 9 oz / 2 cups strawberries,
hulled and chopped
250 g / 9 oz / 2 cups raspberries
250 g / 9 oz / 2 cups redcurrants
250 g / 9 oz / 2 cups cranberries
900 g / 2 lb / 4 cups granulated sugar
568 ml / 1 pint / 2 ¼ cups water
1 tbsp butter

METHOD

Preheat the oven to 170°C (150° fan) / 325F / gas 3.

Place a couple of saucers in the freezer; they will be needed for testing the jam's setting point.

Combine the strawberries, raspberries, redcurrants, cranberries and water in a large saucepan and cook over a medium heat, stirring occasionally, until the fruit softens.

Once soft, add the sugar and stir well, scraping down the sides of the saucepan.

Reduce the heat and simmer the fruit and sugar for 10-15 minutes until the sugar has dissolved, stirring the jam occasionally.

Once the sugar has dissolved, increase the heat and boil the jam for 10 minutes.

Remove the saucepan from the heat and spoon a teaspoon of the hot jam onto the cold saucers from the freezer; when the jam has cooled, prod it to see if a skin has formed. If it has, the jam is ready. If not, continue boiling for a few more minutes before testing again.

Once the jam is ready to set, add the butter and stir well until dissolved into the jam.

Place the jars in the oven with the lids to sterilise them.

Remove after 10 minutes and place on a flat, heatproof surface.

Spoon the jam into the jars and cover their tops with a waxed disc.

Seal well and let the jars cool to room temperature before serving.

Makes: two 500 g jars | Preparation time : 10 minutes | Cooking time : 30-35 minutes

Pear and Cider Jam

INGREDIENTS

1 kg / 2 lb 4 oz / 3 ⅓ cups pears, peeled, cored and diced
250 g / 9 oz / 1 cup caster (superfine) sugar
1 vanilla pod, split in half with seeds scraped out
300 ml / 10 ½ oz / 1 ⅓ cups perry
300 ml / 10 ½ oz / 1 ⅓ cups apple cider
1 tbsp unsalted butter

METHOD

Preheat the oven to 170°C (150° fan) / 325F / gas 3.

Place a couple of saucers in the freezer; they will be needed for testing the jam's setting point.

Combine the pear, perry, cider and vanilla seeds in a large, heavy-based saucepan and cook over a moderate heat until the liquid starts to bubble.

Reduce the heat and simmer the fruit for 8-10 minutes until the fruit is soft enough to crush with the back of a wooden spoon and the liquid has reduced by at least half.

Add the sugar at this point and puree with a stick blender so that you have a smooth jam; you can retain some texture if desired.

Simmer for another 5-10 minutes until the sugar has dissolved.

Increase the heat to boiling point for ten minutes, stirring occasionally.

Remove the saucepan from the heat and spoon a teaspoon of the hot jam onto the cold saucers from the freezer; when the jam has cooled, prod it to see if a skin has formed. If it has, the jam is ready. If not, continue boiling for a few more minutes before testing again.

Once the jam is ready to set, add the butter and stir well until dissolved into the jam.

Place the jars in the oven to sterilise.

Remove after 10 minutes and place on a flat, heatproof surface.

Spoon the jam into the jars and cover their tops with a waxed disc.

Seal with jam muslin and tie well to secure.

Let the jam cool to room temperature before serving.

Makes: **two 500 g jars** | Preparation time : **15 minutes** | Cooking time : **40-45 minutes**

Raspberry Jam

INGREDIENTS

900 g / 2 lb / 7 cups raspberries
1 kg / 2 lb 4 oz / 4 ½ cups granulated sugar
568 ml / 1 pint / 2 ¼ cups water
1 tbsp butter

METHOD

Preheat the oven to 170°C (150° fan) / 325F / gas 3.

Place a couple of saucers in the freezer; they will be needed for testing the jam's setting point.

Combine the raspberries and water in a large saucepan and cook over a medium heat, stirring occasionally, until the fruit softens.

Once soft, add the sugar and stir well, scraping down the sides of the saucepan.

Reduce the heat and simmer the fruit and sugar for 10-15 minutes until the sugar has dissolved, stirring the jam occasionally.

Once the sugar has dissolved, increase the heat and boil the jam for 10 minutes.

Remove the saucepan from the heat and spoon a teaspoon of the hot jam onto the cold saucers from the freezer; when the jam has cooled, prod it to see if a skin has formed. If it has, the jam is ready. If not, continue boiling for a few more minutes before testing again.

Once the jam is ready to set, add the butter and stir well until dissolved into the jam.

Place the jars in the oven with their lids to sterilise them.

Remove after 10 minutes and place on a flat, heatproof surface.

Spoon the jam into the jars and cover their tops with a waxed disc.

Seal well and let the jars cool to room temperature before serving.

Makes: two 500 g jars | Preparation time : 10 minutes | Cooking time : 30-35 minutes

Redcurrant Jam

INGREDIENTS

450 g / 1 lb / 4 cups redcurrants
450 g / 1 lb / 2 cups granulated sugar

METHOD

Place the redcurrants in a large stainless steel saucepan and cook over a moderate heat for 8-10 minutes, stirring and breaking the fruit with a spoon as it softens.

Once the juice has been released from them, increase the heat and simmer for 5 minutes, then add the sugar, stirring well.

Increase the heat again and boil the mixture for 6 minutes.

Line a sieve with a double layer of muslin and strain the mixture though it into a bowl underneath.

As the mixture is draining, preheat the oven to 170°C (150° fan) / 325F / gas 3.

Place the jar in the oven with its lid to sterilise.

Remove after 10 minutes and fill with the hot jam.

Seal immediately and cover the top with a waxed disc.

Let it cool to room temperature before chilling or serving.

Makes: one 500 g jar | Preparation time : 5 minutes | Cooking time : 25-30 minutes

Blueberry Jam

INGREDIENTS

450 g / 1 lb / 3 ½ cups blueberries
500 g / 1 lb 2 oz / 2 ¼ cups granulated
sugar
250 ml / 9 fl. oz / 1 cup water
1 tsp butter

METHOD

Preheat the oven to 170°C (150° fan) / 325F / gas 3.

Place a couple of saucers in the freezer; they will be needed for testing the jam's setting point.

Combine the blueberries and water in a large saucepan and cook over a medium heat, stirring occasionally, until the fruit softens.

Once soft, add the sugar and stir well, scraping down the sides of the saucepan.

Reduce the heat and simmer the fruit and sugar for 8-10 minutes until the sugar has dissolved, stirring the jam occasionally.

Once the sugar has dissolved, increase the heat and boil the jam for 7 minutes.

Remove the saucepan from the heat and spoon a teaspoon of the hot jam onto the cold saucers from the freezer; when the jam has cooled, prod it to see if a skin has formed. If it has, the jam is ready. If not, continue boiling for a few more minutes before testing again.

Once the jam is ready to set, add the butter and stir well until dissolved into the jam.

Place the jar in the oven with its lid to sterilise.

Remove after 10 minutes and place on a flat, heatproof surface.

Spoon the jam into the jar and cover the top with a waxed disc.

Seal well and let the jar cool to room temperature before serving.

Makes: one 500 g jar | Preparation time : 5 minutes | Cooking time : 25-30 minutes

Blackberry Jam

INGREDIENTS

900 g / 2 lb / 7 cups blackberries
1 kg / 2 lb 4 oz / 4 ½ cups granulated sugar
568 ml / 1 pint / 2 ¼ cups water
1 tbsp butter

METHOD

Preheat the oven to 170°C (150° fan) / 325F / gas 3.

Place a couple of saucers in the freezer; they will be needed for testing the jam's setting point.

Combine the blackberries and water in a large saucepan and cook over a medium heat, stirring occasionally, until the fruit softens.

Once soft, add the sugar and stir well, scraping down the sides of the saucepan.

Reduce the heat and simmer the fruit and sugar for 10-15 minutes until the sugar has dissolved, stirring the jam occasionally.

Once the sugar has dissolved, increase the heat and boil the jam for 10 minutes.

Remove the saucepan from the heat and spoon a teaspoon of the hot jam onto the cold saucers from the freezer; when the jam has cooled, prod it to see if a skin has formed. If it has, the jam is ready. If not, continue boiling for a few more minutes before testing again.

Once the jam is ready to set, add the butter and stir well until dissolved into the jam.

Place the jars in the oven with their lids to sterilise them.

Remove after 10 minutes and place on a flat, heatproof surface.

Spoon the jam into the jars and cover their tops with a waxed disc.

Seal well and let the jars cool to room temperature before serving.

Makes: **two 500 g jars** | Preparation time : **10 minutes** | Cooking time : **30-35 minutes**

Rhubarb Jam

INGREDIENTS

900 g / 2 lb / 7 cups rhubarb, peeled and chopped
1 kg / 2 lb 4 oz / 4 ½ cups granulated sugar
568 ml / 1 pint / 2 ¼ cups water
1 orange, juiced
½ tsp ground ginger
1 tbsp butter

METHOD

Preheat the oven to 170°C (150° fan) / 325F / gas 3.

Place a couple of saucers in the freezer; they will be needed for testing the jam's setting point.

Combine the rhubarb, ginger, orange juice and water in a large saucepan and cook over a medium heat, stirring occasionally, until the fruit softens.

Once soft, add the sugar and stir well, scraping down the sides of the saucepan.

Reduce the heat and simmer the fruit and sugar for 10-15 minutes until the sugar has dissolved, stirring the jam occasionally.

Once the sugar has dissolved, increase the heat and boil the jam for 10 minutes.

Remove the saucepan from the heat and spoon a teaspoon of the hot jam onto the cold saucers from the freezer; when the jam has cooled, prod it to see if a skin has formed. If it has, the jam is ready. If not, continue boiling for a few more minutes before testing again.

Once the jam is ready to set, add the butter and stir well until dissolved into the jam.

Place the jars in the oven with their lids to sterilise them.

Remove after 10 minutes and place on a flat, heatproof surface.

Spoon the jam into the jars and cover their tops with a waxed disc.

Seal well and let the jars cool to room temperature before serving.

Makes: two 500 g jars | Preparation time : 10 minutes | Cooking time : 30-35 minutes

Apricot and Hazelnut Jam

INGREDIENTS

1 kg / 2 lb 4 oz / 5 cups apricots,
de-stoned and roughly chopped
700 g / 1 lb 9 oz / 3 cups granulated
sugar
225 g / 8 oz / 1 ½ cups hazelnuts,
blanched and finely chopped

METHOD

Combine the apricot and sugar in a large mixing bowl.

Toss well and cover with a tea towel before leaving overnight.

The next day, place a couple of saucers in the freezer; they will be needed for testing the jam's setting point.

Preheat the oven to 170°C (150° fan) / 325F / gas 3.

Place the jars in the oven for 10 minutes to sterilise, with their lids.

Place the fruit and sugar mixture in a large stainless steel saucepan and cook over a high heat for 15 minutes, stirring occasionally.

Remove the saucepan from the heat and spoon a teaspoon of the hot jam onto the cold saucers from the freezer; when the jam has cooled, prod it to see if a skin has formed. If it has, the jam is ready. If not, continue boiling for a few more minutes before testing again.

Once the jam is ready to set, add the butter and stir well until dissolved into the jam.

Spoon some of the hot jam into the jars so that it fills roughly half of them.

Sprinkle over half of the chopped hazelnuts in an even layer, then cover with more jam, filling the jars almost to their tops.

Sprinkle the remaining chopped hazelnuts on top in another even layer.

Cover the tops with a waxed disc before sealing well.

Let the jam cool to room temperature before using or storing.

Makes: two 500 g jars | Preparation time : 15-20 minutes | Cooking time : 25-30 minutes

Dandelion and Marigold Jam

INGREDIENTS

6 large oranges
small handful of dandelion petals
small handful of marigold petals
225 g / 8 oz / 1 cup honey
225 g / 8 oz / 1 cup granulated sugar

METHOD

Peel the skin from half of the oranges using a vegetable peeler.

Julienne the zest and reserve to one side.

Halve and squeeze the oranges into a measuring jug; remove all the pulp and pips but reserve them.

Pour the juice into a large non-metallic bowl.

Make the juice from the oranges up to 1.7 l with cold water.

Place the pulp and pips on a sheet of muslin and tie up into a bag using kitchen twine or string.

Place in the orange liquid along with the zest, then cover the bowl and leave it overnight.

The next day, pour the liquid and the muslin bag into a large, stainless steel saucepan and cook over a medium heat for 25-30 minutes until the peel is soft.

Preheat the oven to 170°C (150° fan) / 325F / gas 3.

Place a couple of saucers in the freezer; they will be needed for testing the jam's setting point.

Place the jars with their lids in the oven for 10 minutes, to sterilise.

Remove the muslin bag and keep to one side until cool enough to handle.

Add the sugar and honey to the saucepan and stir well, then squeeze all the liquid contents from the muslin bag back into the saucepan.

Boil the jam for 10 minutes, and then remove the saucepan from the heat and spoon a teaspoon of the hot jam onto the cold saucers from the freezer. When the jam has cooled, prod it to see if a skin has formed. If so, it is ready. If not, continue boiling for 3-4 minutes before testing again.

When ready, remove the pan from the heat and stir through the flower petals. Fill the sterilised jars with the hot jam and seal immediately.

Let the jam cool to room temperature before serving.

Makes: two 500 g jars | Preparation time : 15 minutes | Cooking time : 60 minutes

Elderberry and Plum Jam

INGREDIENTS

250 g / 9 oz / 2 cups elderberries
6 plums, de-stoned and roughly
chopped
450 g / 1 lb / 2 cups granulated sugar
250 ml / 9 fl. oz / 1 cup water
1 tsp butter

METHOD

Preheat the oven to 170°C (150° fan) / 325F / gas 3.

Place a couple of saucers in the freezer; they will be needed for testing the jam's setting point.

Combine the elderberries, plums and water in a large saucepan.

Cook over a medium heat, stirring occasionally, until the fruit softens.

Once soft, add the sugar to both and stir well, scraping down the sides of the saucepan.

Reduce the heat and simmer the fruits and sugar for 10-15 minutes until the sugar has dissolved, stirring the jam occasionally.

Once the sugar has dissolved, increase the heat and boil the jam for 10 minutes.

Remove the saucepans from the heat and spoon a teaspoon of the hot jam onto the cold saucers from the freezer; when the jam has cooled, prod it to see if a skin has formed. If it has, the jam is ready. If not, continue boiling for a few more minutes before testing again.

Once the jam is ready to set, add the butter and stir well until dissolved into the jam.

Place the jar in the oven with its lid to sterilise it.

Remove after 10 minutes and place on a flat, heatproof surface.

Spoon the jam into the jar and cover the top with a waxed disc.

Seal well and let the jam cool to room temperature before serving.

Makes: one 500 g jar | Preparation time : 15 minutes | Cooking time : 30-35 minutes

Peach and Raspberry Jam

INGREDIENTS

900 g / 2 lb / 4 cups peaches, de-stoned and diced
450 g / 1 lb / 3 ½ cups raspberries
900 g / 2 lb / 4 cups granulated sugar
568 ml / 1 pint / 2 ¼ cups water
1 tsp natural red food colouring
1 tbsp unsalted butter

METHOD

Preheat the oven to 170°C (150° fan) / 325F / gas 3.

Place a couple of saucers in the freezer; they will be needed for testing the jam's setting point.

Combine the raspberries, food colouring and water in a large saucepan and cook over a medium heat, stirring occasionally, until the fruit softens.

Once soft, add the sugar and peach and stir well, scraping down the sides of the saucepan.

Reduce the heat and simmer the fruit and sugar for 10-15 minutes until the sugar has dissolved, stirring the jam occasionally.

Once the sugar has dissolved, increase the heat and boil the jam for 10 minutes.

Remove the saucepan from the heat and spoon a teaspoon of the hot jam onto the cold saucers from the freezer; when the jam has cooled, prod it to see if a skin has formed. If it has, the jam is ready. If not, continue boiling for a few more minutes and then test again.

Once the jam is ready to set, add the butter and stir well until dissolved into the jam.

Place the jars in the oven for 10 minutes to sterilise, then remove and place on a flat, heatproof surface.

Spoon the hot jam into the jars and cover their tops with a waxed disc.

Seal well and let the jars cool to room temperature before serving.

Makes: two 500 g jars | Preparation time : 10-15 minutes | Cooking time : 35-40 minutes

Grapefruit and Honey Jam

INGREDIENTS

6 large pink grapefruit, halved
2 large oranges, halved
450 g / 1 lb / 2 cups honey
450 g / 1 lb / 2 cups granulated sugar
6" root ginger, peeled and very
finely grated

METHOD

Peel the skin from half of the grapefruit using a vegetable peeler. Julienne the zest and reserve to one side.

Squeeze the grapefruit and oranges into a measuring jug; remove all the pulp and pips but reserve them.

Pour the juice into a large non-metallic bowl.

Make the juice from the fruit up to 3.4 l using cold water.

Place the pulp and pips on a sheet of muslin and tie up into a bag using kitchen twine or string.

Place in the grapefruit liquid along with the grated ginger and the reserved zest, then cover the bowl and leave it overnight.

The next day, pour the liquid and the muslin bag into a saucepan and cook over a medium heat for 40-45 minutes until the peel is soft.

Preheat the oven to 170°C (150° fan) / 325F / gas 3.

Place a couple of saucers in the freezer; they will be needed for testing the jam's setting point.

Place the jars with their lids in the oven for 10 minutes, to sterilise.

Remove the muslin bag and keep to one side.

Add the sugar and honey to the saucepan and stir well, then squeeze all the liquid contents from the muslin bag back into the saucepan.

Boil the jam for 15 minutes, and then remove from the heat and spoon a teaspoon of the hot jam onto the one of cold saucers from the freezer.

When the jam has cooled, prod it to see if a skin has formed. If so, it is ready. If not, continue boiling for 3-4 minutes before testing again.

When ready, remove the pan from the heat and set it to one side.

Fill the sterilised jars with the hot jam and seal immediately.

Let the jam cool to room temperature before serving.

Makes: four 500 g jars | Preparation time : 15-20 minutes | Cooking time : 1 hour 10 minutes

Lemon Curd

INGREDIENTS

225 g / 8 oz / 1 cup caster
(superfine) sugar
30 g / 1 oz / 2 tbsp cornflour
125 ml / 4 ½ fl. oz / ½ cup lemon juice
125 ml / 4 ½ fl. oz / ½ cup lime juice
150 ml / 5 fl. oz / ⅔ cup water
175 g / 6 oz / 1 ½ sticks butter, cubed
6 mediums egg yolks
2 medium eggs

METHOD

Preheat the oven to 170°C (150° fan) / 325F / gas 3.

Combine the cornflour and sugar in a saucepan.

Gradually add the lemon and lime juice, whisking as you pour,
then add the water.

Cook over a medium heat, stirring constantly until it thickens.

Once the mixture starts to bubble, remove from the heat and beat
in the butter, one cube at a time, until incorporated.

Whisk together the eggs and egg yolks in a separate jug and beat into
the mixture.

Return to the heat and stir constantly for 4-6 minutes until the mixture
drops from a spoon with a light tap.

Remove from the heat and let it cool slightly.

Place the jar in the oven for 10 minutes to sterilise.

Remove the jar from the oven and fill with the warm lemon curd.

Seal well and let the curd cool to room temperature before storing
in the fridge.

Makes: one 500 g jar | Preparation time : 10-15 minutes | Cooking time : 15-20 minutes

Ginger and Peach Jam

INGREDIENTS

900 g / 2 lb / 4 ½ cups, peaches
de-stoned and diced
1 kg / 2 lb 4 oz / 4 ½ cups granulated
sugar
568 ml / 1 pint / 2 ¼ cups water
6" ginger, peeled and finely grated
½ tsp ground ginger
1 tbsp butter

METHOD

Preheat the oven to 170°C (150° fan) / 325F / gas 3.

Place a couple of saucers in the freezer; they will be needed for testing the jam's setting point.

Combine the peach, ginger, ground ginger and water in a large saucepan and cook over a medium heat, stirring occasionally, until the fruit softens.

Once soft, add the sugar and stir well, scraping down the sides of the saucepan.

Reduce the heat and simmer the fruit and sugar for 10-15 minutes until the sugar has dissolved, stirring the jam occasionally.

Once the sugar has dissolved, increase the heat and boil the jam for 10 minutes.

Remove the saucepan from the heat and spoon a teaspoon of the hot jam onto the cold saucers from the freezer; when the jam has cooled, prod it to see if a skin has formed. If it has, the jam is ready. If not, continue boiling for a few more minutes before testing again.

Once the jam is ready to set, add the butter and stir well until dissolved into the jam.

Place the jars in the oven with their lids to sterilise them.

Remove after 10 minutes and place on a flat, heatproof surface.

Spoon the jam into the jars and cover their tops with a waxed disc.

Seal well and let the jars cool to room temperature before serving.

Makes: two 500 g jars | Preparation time : 10 minutes | Cooking time : 30-35 minutes

Wild Fruit Jam

INGREDIENTS

450 g / 1 lb / 2 cups apples, peeled, cored and finely diced
200 g / 10 ½ oz / 1 ⅓ cups blackberries
150 g / 5 oz / 1 cup bilberries
110 g / 4 oz / ⅔ cup redcurrants
675 g / 1 lb 8 oz / 3 cups caster (superfine) sugar
568 ml / 1 pint / 2 ¼ cups water
1 tbsp unsalted butter

METHOD

Preheat the oven to 170°C (150° fan) / 325F / gas 3.

Place a couple of saucers in the freezer; they will be needed for testing the jam's setting point.

Combine all the fruits with the water in a large saucepan and cook over a medium heat, stirring occasionally, until the apples soften.

Once soft, add the sugar and stir well, scraping down the sides of the saucepan.

Reduce the heat and simmer the fruit and sugar for 10 minutes until the sugar has dissolved, stirring the jam occasionally.

Once the sugar has dissolved, increase the heat and boil the jam for 10 minutes; stirring from time to time to help break up the fruit.

Remove the saucepan from the heat and spoon a teaspoon of the hot jam onto the cold saucers from the freezer; when the jam has cooled, prod it to see if a skin has formed. If it has, the jam is ready. If not, continue boiling for a few more minutes before testing again.

Once the jam is ready to set, add the butter and stir well until incorporated.

Place the two jars in the oven with the lids to sterilise them.

Remove after 10 minutes and place on a flat, heatproof surface.

Spoon the jam into the jars and cover their tops with a waxed disc.

Seal well and let the jars cool to room temperature before serving.

Makes: two 500 g jars | Preparation time : 15 minutes | Cooking time : 35-45 minutes

Berry and Currant Jam

INGREDIENTS

450 g / 1 lb / 3 ½ cups blackcurrants, washed
450 g / 1 lb / 3 ½ cups raspberries, washed
1 kg / 2 lb 4 oz / 4 ½ cups granulated sugar
568 ml / 1 pint / 2 ¼ cups water
1 tbsp butter

METHOD

Preheat the oven to 170°C (150° fan) / 325F / gas 3.

Place a couple of saucers in the freezer; they will be needed for testing the jam's setting point.

Combine the blackcurrants, raspberries and water in a large saucepan and cook over a medium heat, stirring occasionally, until the fruit softens.

Once soft, add the sugar and stir well, scraping down the sides of the saucepan.

Reduce the heat and simmer the fruit and sugar for 10-15 minutes until the sugar has dissolved, stirring the jam occasionally.

Once the sugar has dissolved, increase the heat and boil the jam for 10 minutes.

Remove the saucepan from the heat and spoon a teaspoon of the hot jam onto the cold saucers from the freezer; when the jam has cooled, prod it to see if a skin has formed. If it has, the jam is ready. If not, continue boiling for a few more minutes before testing again.

Once the jam is ready to set, add the butter and stir well until dissolved into the jam.

Place the two jars in the oven with their lids to sterilise them.

Remove after 10 minutes and place on a flat, heatproof surface.

Spoon the jam into the jars and cover their tops with a waxed disc.

Seal well and let the jars cool to room temperature before serving.

Makes: two 500 g jars | Preparation time : 10 minutes | Cooking time : 30-35 minutes

Apricot and Pear Jam

INGREDIENTS

500 g / 1 lb 2 oz / 2 ½ cups fresh apricots, de-stoned and roughly chopped
500 g / 1 lb 2 oz / 2 ½ cups pears, cored and roughly chopped
700 g / 1 lb 9 oz / 3 cups granulated sugar

METHOD

Combine the apricot, pear and sugar in a large mixing bowl.

Toss well and cover with a tea towel before leaving overnight.

The next day, place a couple of saucers in the freezer; they will be needed for testing the jam's setting point.

Preheat the oven to 170°C (150° fan) / 325F / gas 3.

Place the jars in the oven for 10 minutes to sterilise, with their lids.

Place the fruit and sugar mixture in a large stainless steel saucepan and cook over a high heat for 15 minutes, stirring occasionally.

Remove the saucepan from the heat and spoon a teaspoon of the hot jam onto the cold saucers from the freezer; when the jam has cooled, prod it to see if a skin has formed. If it has, the jam is ready. If not, continue boiling for a few more minutes before testing again.

Once the jam is ready to set, add the butter and stir well until dissolved into the jam.

Spoon the hot jam into the sterilised jars, then cover with a waxed disc and seal well.

Let the jam cool to room temperature before using or storing.

Makes: two 500 g jars | Preparation time : 15-20 minutes | Cooking time : 20-25 minutes

Chestnut Jam

INGREDIENTS

550 ml / 1 pint / 2 ⅓ cups whole milk
450 g / 1 lb / 3 cups cooked chestnuts, finely chopped
110 g / 4 oz / ½ cup sweetened chestnut purée
1 tsp vanilla extract

METHOD

Preheat the oven to 170°C (150° fan) / 325F / gas 3.

Place the jar in the oven with its lid to sterilise for 10 minutes.

Place the cooked chestnuts in a saucepan and cover with the milk and vanilla extract.

Simmer for 10 minutes, then drain and transfer the chestnuts to a food processor.

Add the chestnut purée and some of the milk and pulse the mixture until it comes together to form a smooth jam.

Add a little more milk if you need to loosen the jam.

Remove the jar from the oven and fill with the jam.

Seal well and let it cool to room temperature before serving.

Makes: one 500 g jar | Preparation time : 10 minutes | Cooking time : 15-20 minutes

Cranberry Jam

INGREDIENTS

250 ml / 9 fl. oz / 1 cup water
450 g / 1 lb / 4 cups cranberries
225 g / 8 oz / 1 cup granulated sugar
1 lemon, juiced

METHOD

Place all the ingredients in a large stainless steel pan and cover with the water.

Simmer the mixture over a medium heat, stirring occasionally, until the sugar has dissolved and the cranberries are soft.

Increase the heat and boil the jam for 10 minutes until two-thirds of the liquid has evaporated away.

Remove from the heat and set to one side.

Preheat the oven to 170°C (150° fan) / 325F / gas 3.

Place the jar in the oven to sterilise, with its lid.

Remove after 10 minutes and fill with the hot jam.

Seal well, then allow it to cool to room temperature and store in the fridge.

Makes: **one 500 g jar** | Preparation time : **5 minutes** | Cooking time : **25-30 minutes**

Cherry and Orange Jam

INGREDIENTS

900 g / 2 lb / 4 ½ cups cherries, de-stoned and washed
2 large oranges, juiced
1 kg / 2 lb 4 oz / 4 ½ cups granulated sugar
400 ml / 14 fl. oz / 1 ⅗ cups water
1 tbsp butter

METHOD

Preheat the oven to 170°C (150° fan) / 325F / gas 3.

Place a couple of saucers in the freezer; they will be needed for testing the jam's setting point.

Combine the cherries, orange juice and water in a large saucepan and cook over a medium heat, stirring occasionally, until the fruit softens.

Once soft, add the sugar and stir well, scraping down the sides of the saucepan.

Reduce the heat and simmer the fruit and sugar for 10-15 minutes until the sugar has dissolved, stirring the jam occasionally.

Once the sugar has dissolved, increase the heat and boil the jam for 10 minutes.

Remove the saucepan from the heat and spoon a teaspoon of the hot jam onto the cold saucers from the freezer; when the jam has cooled, prod it to see if a skin has formed. If it has, the jam is ready. If not, continue boiling for a few more minutes before testing again.

Once the jam is ready to set, add the butter and stir well until dissolved into the jam.

Place the two jars in the oven with their lids to sterilise them.

Remove after 10 minutes and place on a flat, heatproof surface.

Spoon the jam into the jars and cover their tops with a waxed disc.

Seal well and let the jars cool to room temperature before serving.

Makes: two 500 g jars | Preparation time : 15-20 minutes | Cooking time : 30-35 minutes

Banana Jam

INGREDIENTS

900 g / 2 lb / 3 cups bananas, mashed
525 g / 1 lb 3 oz / 3 cups soft
brown sugar
300 ml / 10 ½ fl. oz / 1 ⅓ cup water
2 limes, juiced
1 tsp ground cinnamon
1 tsp vanilla extract

METHOD

Combine the sugar, lime juice, cinnamon, vanilla extract and water
in a large stainless steel saucepan.

Cook over a medium heat, stirring occasionally, until the liquid turns
into a syrup.

Add the mashed banana, stir well, and cook for a further 20-25 minutes
over a slightly reduced heat.

Stir the jam from time to time.

Remove the jam once golden in colour and thickened and set
to one side.

Preheat the oven to 170°C (150° fan) / 325F / gas 3.

Place the jars in the oven, with their lids, to sterilise.

Remove after 10 minutes and fill with the banana jam.

Seal immediately and let the jam cool to room temperature before
serving or storing.

Makes: two 500 g jars | Preparation time : 10-15 minutes | Cooking time : 30-35 minutes

Chocolate Spread

INGREDIENTS

450 g / 1 lb / 3 cups blanched hazelnuts
(cob nuts), lightly toasted
185 g / 6 ½ oz / 1 ½ cups icing
(confectioner's) sugar
75 g / 3 oz / ½ cup cocoa powder
110 ml / 4 fl. oz / ½ cup groundnut oil
½ tsp vanilla extract

METHOD

Pulse the hazelnuts in a food processor until finely ground.

Keep blitzing the nuts until they start to liquefy, about 5 minutes, scraping down the sides from time to time.

Add the sugar, cocoa powder and vanilla extract and pulse to combine.

Keep the motor running and add the oil in a slow, steady drizzle until the mixture is spreadable and of the desired consistency; you might not need to use all of the oil.

Spoon into an airtight container and seal well.

Keep at room temperature to prevent it from hardening.

Makes: one 500 g jar | Preparation time : 10-15 minutes | Cooking time : 10 minutes

Rhubarb and Strawberry Jam

INGREDIENTS

675 g / 1 lb 8 oz / 6 cups strawberries,
hulled and roughly chopped
225 g / 8 oz / 2 cups rhubarb,
peeled and roughly chopped
1 kg / 2 lb 4 oz / 4 ½ cups granulated
sugar
568 ml / 1 pint / 2 ¼ cups water
1 tbsp butter

METHOD

Preheat the oven to 170°C (150° fan) / 325F / gas 3.

Place a couple of saucers in the freezer; they will be needed for testing the jam's setting point.

Combine the strawberries, rhubarb and water in a large saucepan and cook over a medium heat, stirring occasionally, until the fruit softens.

Once soft, add the sugar and stir well, scraping down the sides of the saucepan.

Reduce the heat and simmer the fruit and sugar for 10-15 minutes until the sugar has dissolved, stirring the jam occasionally.

Once the sugar has dissolved, increase the heat and boil the jam for 10 minutes.

Remove the saucepan from the heat and spoon a teaspoon of the hot jam onto one of the cold saucers from the freezer. When the jam has cooled, prod it to see if a skin has formed. If it has, the jam is ready. If not, continue boiling for a few more minutes before testing again.

Once the jam is ready to set, add the butter and stir well until dissolved into the jam.

Place the jars in the oven with their lids to sterilise them.

Remove after 10 minutes and place on a flat, heatproof surface.

Spoon the jam into the jars and cover their tops with a waxed disc.

Seal well and let the jars cool to room temperature before serving.

Makes: two 500 g jars | Preparation time : 10 minutes | Cooking time : 30-35 minutes

Melon Jam

INGREDIENTS

1 cantaloupe melon, peeled and diced
450 g / 2 lb / 2 cups granulated sugar
500 ml / 18 fl. oz / 2 cups cold water
1 lime, juiced
2 vanilla pods, halved without seeds
1 tsp whole cloves

METHOD

Place the sugar, water, lime juice, vanilla pods and cloves in a large stainless steel saucepan.

Cook over a moderate heat, stirring occasionally, until a syrup texture forms.

Add the melon and stir well.

Cook for 10 minutes until the melon is soft enough to mash.

Remove the melon using a slotted spoon and transfer to a food processor.

Purée until smooth and then whisk back into the syrup.

Preheat the oven to 170°C (150° fan) / 325F / gas 3.

Place the jar in the oven and sterilise for 10 minutes.

Remove from the oven and place on a heatproof surface.

Pour the jam into the jar and cover the top with a waxed disc.

Seal immediately and let the jam cool to room temperature before serving or storing.

Makes: one 500 g jar | Preparation time : 10-15 minutes | Cooking time : 25-30 minutes

Morello Cherry Jam

INGREDIENTS

450 g / 1 lb / 2 ¼ cups Morello cherries,
washed and de-stoned
2 large oranges, juiced
450 g / 2 lb / 2 cups granulated sugar
400 ml / 14 fl. oz / 1 ⅔ cups water
1 tbsp butter

METHOD

Preheat the oven to 170°C (150° fan) / 325F / gas 3.

Place a couple of saucers in the freezer; they will be needed for testing the jam's setting point.

Combine the cherries and water in a large saucepan and cook over a medium heat, stirring occasionally, until they soften.

Once soft, add the sugar and stir well, scraping down the sides of the saucepan.

Reduce the heat and simmer the fruit and sugar for 10-15 minutes until the sugar has dissolved, stirring the jam occasionally.

Once the sugar has dissolved, increase the heat and boil the jam for 10 minutes.

Remove the saucepan from the heat and spoon a teaspoon of the hot jam onto the cold saucers from the freezer. When the jam has cooled, prod it to see if a skin has formed. If it has, the jam is ready. If not, continue boiling for a few more minutes before testing again.

Once the jam is ready to set, add the butter and stir well until dissolved into the jam.

Place the jar in the oven with its lids to sterilise.

Remove after 10 minutes and place on a flat, heatproof surface.

Spoon the jam into the jar and cover the top with a waxed disc.

Seal well and let the jar cool to room temperature before serving.

Makes: one 500 g jar | Preparation time : 15-20 minutes | Cooking time : 30-35 minutes

Peach and Kiwi Jam

INGREDIENTS

450 g / 1 lb / 2 ¼ cups peaches,
de-stoned and diced
450 g / 1 lb / 2 ¼ cups kiwi fruit,
peeled and diced
1 kg / 2 lb 4 oz / 4 ½ cups granulated
sugar
568 ml / 1 pint / 2 ¼ cups water
1 tbsp butter

METHOD

Preheat the oven to 170°C (150°C fan) / 325°F / gas 3.

Combine the peach, kiwi and water in a large saucepan and cook over a medium heat, stirring occasionally, until the fruit softens.

Once soft, add the sugar and stir well, scraping down the sides of the saucepan.

Reduce the heat and simmer the fruit and sugar for 10-15 minutes until the sugar has dissolved, stirring the jam occasionally.

Once the sugar has dissolved, increase the heat and boil the jam for 4-5 minutes.

After 10 minutes, stir in the butter until incorporated and roughly purée using a stick blender before setting to one side.

Place the jars in the oven with their lids to sterilise them.

Remove after 10 minutes and place on a flat, heatproof surface.

Spoon the jam into the jars and cover their tops with a waxed disc.

Seal well and let the jars cool to room temperature before serving.

Makes: two 500 g jars | Preparation time : 15-20 minutes | Cooking time : 25-30 minutes

Chutneys

Bell Pepper Chutney

INGREDIENTS

30 ml / 1 fl. oz / 2 tbsp olive oil
2 large red peppers, de-seeded
and finely diced
2 large green peppers, de-seeded
and finely diced
2 large yellow peppers, de-seeded
and finely diced
1 large onion, finely diced
250 ml / 9 fl. oz / 1 cup distilled
white vinegar
225 g / 8 oz / 1 cup golden caster
(superfine) sugar
salt and pepper

METHOD

Heat the olive oil in a large, stainless steel saucepan over a medium heat until hot.

Sweat the onion with a little salt for 4-5 minutes, stirring frequently, until softened.

Add the vinegar and sugar, stir well, and then continue cooking until it has dissolved.

Add the peppers and simmer the mixture for 40-45 minutes over a reduced heat until the liquid has evaporated away to leave you with a soft chutney mixture.

Make sure you stir the chutney from time to time as the liquid evaporates away.

Once ready, season the chutney to taste.

Spoon the chutney into the jar and serve warm or cold with the slices of apple on the side.

Makes: one 500 g jar | Preparation time : 10-15 minutes | Cooking time : 50-55 minutes

Apricot and Ginger Chutney

FOR THE CHUTNEY

350 g / 12 oz / 2 ⅓ cups dried
apricot halves
100 g / 3 ½ oz / ½ cup sultanas
110 g / 4 oz / ⅔ cup whole almonds,
blanched
350 g / 12 oz / 1 ½ cups granulated sugar
375 ml / 13 fl. oz / 1 ½ cups distilled
white vinegar
6" ginger, peeled and finely grated
3 onions, finely chopped
1 tsp ground ginger

METHOD

Heat a large stainless steel saucepan over a medium heat until hot.

Combine the sugar and vinegar in the saucepan, stirring occasionally,
until a syrup texture forms.

Add all of the remaining ingredients and simmer the mixture, uncovered
for 45-50 minutes until a moist, thickened chutney forms.

Meanwhile, preheat the oven to 170°C (150° fan) / 325F / gas 3.

Place the jar in the oven with its lid to sterilise for 10 minutes.

Remove and let it cool to one side, then fill the jar with the chutney
once it has finished cooking.

Seal well with the lid and let it cool to room temperature before serving.

Makes: one 500 g jar | Preparation time : 10-15 minutes | Cooking time : 50-55 minutes

Green Tomato Chutney

INGREDIENTS

55 ml / 2 fl. oz / ¼ cup olive oil
2 onions, chopped
900 g / 2 lbs / 4 cups green tomatoes, chopped
225 g / 8 oz / 2 cups green beans, trimmed and chopped
100 g / 3 ½ oz / ½ cup raisins
110 g / 4 oz / ½ cup caster (superfine) sugar
150 ml / 5 fl. oz / ⅔ cup red wine vinegar
1 thread of saffron
salt and pepper

METHOD

Heat the olive oil in a large stainless steel saucepan set over a medium heat.

Sweat the onion with a little salt for 5-6 minutes, stirring frequently, until softened and starting to turn translucent.

Add the chopped green tomatoes, green beans and raisins and continue to cook for 5 minutes, stirring occasionally.

Add the sugar, stir well, then cover with the red wine vinegar and add the saffron thread.

Simmer the mixture for 15-20 minutes, stirring from time to time, until the liquid has reduced and you have a chutney-like consistency.

Preheat the oven to 170°C (150° fan) / 325F / gas 3.

Place the two jars in the oven with their lids to sterilise for 10 minutes.

Adjust the seasoning to taste, then spoon the chutney into the sterilised jars and let them cool to room temperature before sealing and storing.

Makes: two 500 g jars | Preparation time : 10-15 minutes | Cooking time : 25-30 minutes

Onion Chutney

INGREDIENTS

55 g / 2 oz / ½ stick unsalted butter
55 ml / 2 fl. oz / ¼ cup olive oil
900 g / 2 lb / 6 cups white onions, sliced
2 tbsp caster (superfine) sugar
55 ml / 2 fl. oz / ¼ cup white
wine vinegar
salt and pepper

METHOD

Melt the butter together with the olive oil in a large stainless steel saucepan set over a medium heat.

Sweat the sliced onion with a little salt for 15-20 minutes, stirring occasionally.

De-glaze the pan with the white wine vinegar, stirring the base well with a spatula.

Add the sugar, stir well and continue cooking over a reduced heat for 20-25 minutes until the onions are golden brown in colour.

Adjust the seasoning of the chutney to taste.

Preheat the oven to 170°C (150° fan) / 325F / gas 3.

Place the jar in the oven with its lid to sterilise for 10 minutes.

Spoon into the jar and serve warm or cold.

Makes: one 500 g jar | Preparation time : 15 minutes | Cooking time : 35-45 minutes

Mango Curry Chutney

INGREDIENTS

30 ml / 1 fl. oz / 2 tbsp sunflower oil
2 large mangoes, de-stoned and flesh
chopped
1 red chilli, de-seeded and roughly
chopped
75 ml / 3 fl. oz / ⅓ cup distilled
white vinegar
110 g / 4 oz / ½ cup caster (superfine)
sugar
1 tsp turmeric
1 tsp ground coriander
1 tsp Madras curry powder
salt and pepper

METHOD

Heat the sunflower oil in a large, stainless steel saucepan set over
a medium heat until hot.

Add the ground spices and chilli, stir well for 10 seconds, and
then add the vinegar, taking care, as it will start evaporating away.

Add the sugar, stir well, and then simmer the mixture until it forms
a thin syrup.

Add the mango, then reduce the heat and cook the mixture uncovered
for 40-45 minutes until the liquid has reduced by two thirds.

Adjust the seasoning to taste, and then mash the mixture until you
have a chunky texture.

Let the mixture cool to one side.

Preheat the oven to 170°C (150° fan) / 325F / gas 3.

Place the jars in the oven to sterilise with their lids.

Remove after 10 minutes and fill with the warm chutney.

Let the chutney cool to room temperature before sealing and storing.

Makes: two 500 g jars | Preparation time : 10-15 minutes | Cooking time : 45-55 minutes

Cranberry Chutney

INGREDIENTS

450 g / 1 lb / 4 cups cranberries
225 g / 8 oz / 1 cup caster
(superfine) sugar
250 ml / 9 fl. oz / 1 cup water
110 g / 4 oz / ½ cup raisins
1 orange zest, finely grated
a few thyme leaves
pinch of caraway seeds, to garnish

METHOD

Combine the cranberries with the sugar in a large stainless steel saucepan.

Heat over a medium heat, stirring occasionally, until softened.

Once softened, add the water, orange zest and raisins and continue to cook over a reduced heat for 25-30 minutes until the liquid has reduced by half.

Preheat the oven to 170°C (150° fan) / 375F / gas 3.

Place the jars in the oven for 10 minutes, to sterilise.

Add half of the thyme leaves and stir through the mixture, and then remove from the heat.

Spoon into the jars and allow to cool to room temperature before serving or storing.

Garnish with a pinch of the caraway seeds and a pinch of the remaining thyme leaves before serving with crackers.

Keep any remaining chutney in bowls, covered and chilled.

Makes: two 500 g jars | Preparation time : 5-10 minutes | Cooking time : 35-40 minutes

Tomato Chutney

INGREDIENTS

55 ml / 2 fl. oz / ¼ cup olive oil
2 onions, finely chopped
900 g / 2 lbs / 4 cups vine tomatoes, chopped
110 g / 4 oz / ½ cup caster (superfine) sugar
150 ml / 5 fl. oz / ⅔ cup distilled white vinegar
salt and pepper

METHOD

Heat the olive oil in a large stainless steel saucepan set over a medium heat.

Sweat the onion with a little salt for 5-6 minutes, stirring frequently, until softened and starting to turn translucent.

Add the chopped tomatoes and stir well, cooking for a further 10 minutes.

Add the sugar, stir well, and then cover with the vinegar.

Simmer the mixture for 30-35 minutes, stirring from time to time, until the liquid has reduced and you have a chutney-like consistency.

Spoon the chutney into a food processor and pulse until smoother.

Preheat the oven to 170°C (150° fan) / 325F / gas 3.

Place the jars in the oven with their lids to sterilise for 10 minutes.

Adjust the seasoning of the chutney to taste.

Pour into the sterilised jars and let them cool to room temperature before sealing and storing.

Makes: two 500 g jars | Preparation time : 15 minutes | Cooking time : 45-55 minutes

Dried Fruit Chutney

INGREDIENTS

2 large oranges, peeled,
pith and skin removed
150 g / 5 oz / 1 cup dried apricot halves
100 g / 3 ½ oz / ½ cup sultanas
225 g / 8 oz / 1 cup granulated sugar
175 ml / 6 fl. oz / ¾ cup white wine
vinegar
55 g / 2 oz / ½ cup walnut halves,
roughly chopped
1 tsp red chilli flakes
salt and pepper

METHOD

Segment the oranges into chunks.

Heat the sugar in a large, stainless steel saucepan over a moderate heat until it starts to dissolve and caramelise.

Carefully pour the vinegar on top and swirl to combine the two into a gastrique.

Add the dried fruit, oranges chunks, sultanas, walnuts, chilli flakes and a little seasoning and stir well.

Simmer the mixture over a reduced heat for 15-20 minutes until the liquid has evaporated away to leave you with moist chutney.

Season to taste before spooning into serving pots.

Let it cool to room temperature before using. Use within 2-3 days.

Makes: one 500 g jar | Preparation time : 10-15 minutes | Cooking time : 25-30 minutes

Piccalilli Sauce

INGREDIENTS

1 head cauliflower, prepared into small florets

4 large carrots, peeled and finely diced

125 g / 4 ½ oz / 1 cup pickled onions, drained and roughly chopped

125 g / 4 ½ oz / 1 cup gherkins, finely diced

55 g / 2 oz / ¼ cup sea salt

55 g / 2 oz / ⅓ cup English mustard powder

30 g / 1 oz / 2 tbsp plain (all-purpose) flour

1 tbsp turmeric

225 g / 8 oz / 1 cup granulated sugar

900 ml / 1 pint 12 fl. oz / 3 ⅗ cups distilled white vinegar

1.2 l / 2 pints 3 fl. oz / 5 ⅘ cups water

METHOD

Dissolve the salt in the water.

Place all the vegetables in a large, non-metallic bowl and cover with the brine.

Cover the bowl and keep the vegetables submerged in the brine for 24 hours.

Drain the vegetables and rinse well under cold running water.

Cook in a large saucepan of boiling water for 2 minutes, then drain and refresh in iced water.

Preheat the oven to 170°C (150° fan) / 325F / gas 3.

Place the jars in the oven with their lids for 15 minutes.

Combine the turmeric, flour, mustard powder and sugar in a large bowl and add some of the vinegar, whisking well to create a paste.

Add the rest of the vinegar and whisk well, then transfer to a large saucepan and simmer for a few minutes, stirring frequently.

Increase the heat and boil for a few minutes stirring all the time, then return to a simmer and cook for 10 minutes, stirring occasionally.

Add the vegetables to the liquid, and then remove from the heat.

Remove the jars and lids from the oven.

Spoon the sauce into the warm, sterilised jars and seal well before letting them cool to room temperature.

Makes: two 500 g jars | Preparation time : 20-25 minutes | Cooking time : 25-30 minutes

Courgette Chutney

INGREDIENTS

2 large courgettes, finely sliced
2 cloves garlic, crushed
700 ml / 1 pint 5 fl. oz / 3 ⅓ cups olive oil
salt and pepper

METHOD

Place the two jars in the oven with their lids to sterilise.

Combine the olive oil and the garlic in a large stainless steel saucepan.

Warm over a gentle heat for 10 minutes, then remove from the heat and let cool to one side.

Arrange the sliced courgette in a single layer on a tray and season well.

Let the courgette sit for 30 minutes, then pat them dry with kitchen towel.

Preheat the oven to 170°C (150° fan) / 325F / gas 3.

Remove the jars and their lids from the oven after 10 minutes and place on a heatproof mat.

Divide the courgettes evenly between the two jars and cover with the olive oil.

Top up with a little more olive oil if needed, making sure the courgettes are totally submerged.

Let the courgettes and olive oil cool to room temperature before sealing and storing.

Makes: two 500 g jars | Preparation time : 10-15 minutes | Cooking time : 15 minutes

Pear Chutney

INGREDIENTS

2 onions, sliced
6 pears, cored and diced
110 g / 4 oz / ⅔ cup whole almonds,
roughly chopped
110 g / 4 oz / ½ cup caster
(superfine) sugar
100 g / 3 ½ oz / ½ cup raisins
55 ml / 2 fl. oz / ¼ cup distilled
white vinegar
salt

METHOD

Combine the sugar and vinegar in a stainless steel saucepan.

Cook over a low heat, stirring frequently, until the sugar has dissolved.

Add the remaining ingredients apart from the almonds and stir well.

Cover with a lid and cook for 25-30 minutes until the pear and onion are soft.

Meanwhile, preheat the oven to 170°C (150° fan) / 325F / gas 3.

Place the jar in the oven with its lid to sterilise.

Remove after 10 minutes and set to one side.

Add the almonds to the chutney once the fruit and onions are soft and stir well.

Spoon into the sterilised jar and seal immediately.

Let the chutney cool to room temperature before serving or storing.

Makes: one 500 g jar | Preparation time : 10-15 minutes | Cooking time : 30-35 minutes

Aioli Sauce

FOR THE SAUCE

250 ml / 9 fl. oz / 1 cup olive oil
2 cloves of garlic, minced
2 small egg yolks
1 tsp Dijon mustard
1 tbsp lemon juice, to taste
salt and freshly ground pepper
chopped parsley

METHOD

Prepare the aioli by mixing the garlic with salt and pepper in a large mixing bowl.

In a separate mixing bowl, whisk together the egg yolks and mustard until smooth.

Whisk in the oil in a slow, steady drizzle until you have a thickened sauce.

Whisk in the garlic mixture and season with the lemon juice to taste.

Transfer to a serving bowl, cover, and chill until needed.

Garnish the aioli with a sprinkling of chopped parsley before serving.

Makes: **4 portions** | Preparation time : **10 minutes** | Cooking time : **10 minutes**

Yellow Tomato Chutney

INGREDIENTS

55 ml / 2 fl. oz / ¼ cup olive oil
2 onions, chopped
900 g / 2 lbs / 4 cups yellow tomatoes, chopped
110 g / 4 oz / ½ cup caster (superfine) sugar
55 g / 2 oz / ¼ cup sultanas
150 ml / 5 fl. oz / ⅔ cup distilled white vinegar
½ tsp turmeric
salt and pepper

METHOD

Heat the olive oil in a large stainless steel saucepan set over a medium heat.

Sweat the onion with a little salt for 5-6 minutes, stirring frequently, until softened and starting to turn translucent.

Sprinkle over the turmeric and stir well.

Add the chopped yellow tomato and sultanas and continue to cook for 5 minutes, stirring occasionally.

Add the sugar, stir well, and then cover with the vinegar.

Simmer the mixture for 15-20 minutes, stirring from time to time, until the liquid has reduced and you have a chutney-like consistency.

Preheat the oven to 170°C (150° fan) / 325F / gas 3.

Place the jars in the oven with their lids to sterilise, for 10 minutes.

Adjust the seasoning to taste, then spoon the chutney into the sterilised jars and let them cool to room temperature before sealing and storing.

Makes: two 500 g jars | Preparation time : 10-15 minutes | Cooking time : 25-30 minutes

Plum and Ginger Chutney

INGREDIENTS

12 plums, de-stoned and
roughly chopped
225 g / 8 oz / 1 cup granulated sugar
125 ml / 4 ½ fl. oz / ½ cup water
4" ginger, peeled and finely grated
½ tsp vanilla extract

METHOD

Preheat the oven to 170°C (150° fan) / 325F / gas 3.

Combine the plums, ginger, vanilla extract and water in a large saucepan and cook over a medium heat, stirring occasionally, until the fruit softens.

Once soft, add the sugar and stir well, scraping down the sides of the saucepan.

Reduce the heat and simmer the plums, ginger and sugar for 25-30 minutes until thickened and soft, then remove from the heat and purée with a blender until smooth.

Place the jar in the oven with its lid to sterilise.

Remove after 10 minutes and place on a flat, heatproof surface.

Spoon the chutney into the sterilised jar and cover the top with a waxed disc.

Seal well and let the chutney cool to room temperature before serving.

Makes: one 500 g jar | Preparation time : 10-15 minutes | Cooking time : 30-35 minutes

Marmalades

Citrus Marmalade

INGREDIENTS

6 large oranges
6 large lemons
1 kg / 2 lbs 4 oz / 4 ½ cups
granulated sugar

METHOD

Peel half of the oranges and lemons so you are left with thin pieces of peel.

Julienne the peel and reserve to one side.

Squeeze the oranges and lemons into a measuring jug; remove all the pulp and pips but reserve them.

Pour the juice into a large bowl.

Make the juice from the oranges and lemons up to 3 ½ litres with cold water.

Place the pulp and pips on a sheet of muslin and tie up into a bag using kitchen twine or string.

Place in the liquid, then cover the bowl and leave overnight.

The next day, pour the liquid and the muslin bag into a saucepan and cook over a medium heat for 40-45 minutes until the peel is soft.

Preheat the oven to 170°C (150° fan) / 325F / gas 3.

Place a couple of saucers in the freezer; they will be needed for testing the marmalade's setting point.

Place the jars with their lids in the oven for 10 minutes, to sterilise.

Remove the muslin bag and keep to one side until cool enough to handle.

Add the sugar to the saucepan and stir well, then squeeze all the liquid contents from the muslin bag back into the saucepan.

Boil the marmalade for 15 minutes, and then remove from the heat and spoon a teaspoon of the marmalade onto the cold saucers from the freezer; when the marmalade has cooled, prod it to see if a skin has formed. If so, it is ready. If not, continue boiling for 3-4 minutes before testing again.

When ready, remove the pan from the heat and set it to one side.

Fill the jars with the hot marmalade and seal immediately.

Let the marmalade cool to room temperature before serving.

Makes: four 500 g jars | Preparation time : 15-20 minutes | Cooking time : 1 hour 10 minutes

Lemon Marmalade

INGREDIENTS

12 large lemons
500 g / 1 lbs 2 oz / 2 ¼ cups
granulated sugar

METHOD

Peel half of the zest from the lemons so you are left with thin pieces Julienne the peel and reserve to one side.

Squeeze the lemons into a measuring jug; remove all the pulp and pips but reserve them.

Pour the juice into a large bowl. Make the juice up to 1.7 ⅓ pints with cold water.

Place the pulp and pips on a sheet of muslin and tie up into a bag using kitchen twine or string.

Place in the lemon liquid, then cover the bowl and leave it overnight.

The next day, pour the liquid and the muslin bag into a saucepan and cook over a medium heat for 30-35 minutes until the peel is soft.

Preheat the oven to 170°C (150° fan) / 325F / gas 3.

Place a couple of saucers in the freezer; they will be needed for testing the marmalade's setting point.

Place the two jars with their lids in the oven to sterilise.

Remove the muslin bag and keep to one side.

Add the sugar to the saucepan and stir well, then squeeze all the liquid contents from the muslin bag back into the saucepan.

Boil the marmalade for 10-12 minutes, and then remove the saucepan from the heat. Spoon a teaspoon of the hot marmalade onto the cold saucers from the freezer; when the marmalade has cooled, prod it to see if a skin has formed. If so, it is ready. If not, continue boiling for 3-4 minutes before testing again.

When ready, remove the pan from the heat and set it to one side.

Fill the sterilised jars with the hot marmalade and seal immediately.

Let the marmalade cool to room temperature before serving.

Makes: **two 500 jars** | Preparation time : **10 minutes** | Cooking time : **50-55 minutes**

Lime Marmalade

INGREDIENTS

16 large limes
500 g / 1 lbs 2 oz / 2 ¼ cups
granulated sugar

METHOD

Peel half of the limes, then julienne and reserve to one side.

Squeeze the limes into a measuring jug; remove all the pulp and pips but reserve them.

Pour the juice into a large bowl. Make the juice up to 1.7 l with cold water.

Place the pulp and pips on a sheet of muslin and tie up into a bag using kitchen twine or string.

Place in the lime liquid, then cover the bowl and leave it overnight.

The next day, pour the liquid and the muslin bag into a saucepan and cook over a medium heat for 30-35 minutes until the peel is soft.

Preheat the oven to 170°C (150° fan) / 325F / gas 3.

Place a couple of saucers in the freezer; they will be needed for testing the marmalade's setting point. Place the jars with their lids in the oven to sterilise.

Remove the muslin bag and keep to one side.

Add the sugar to the saucepan and stir well, then squeeze all the liquid contents from the muslin bag back into the saucepan.

Boil the marmalade for 10-12 minutes, and then remove the saucepan from the heat and spoon a teaspoon of the hot marmalade onto the cold saucers from the freezer; when the marmalade has cooled, prod it to see if a skin has formed. If so, it is ready. If not, continue boiling for 3-4 minutes before testing again.

When ready, remove the pan from the heat and set it to one side.

Fill the sterilised jars with the hot marmalade and seal immediately.

Let the marmalade cool to room temperature before serving.

Makes: two 500 g jars | Preparation time : 10 minutes | Cooking time : 50-55 minutes

Ginger Marmalade

INGREDIENTS

10 large Seville oranges
1 kg / 2 lbs 4 oz / 4 ½ cups
granulated sugar
12" ginger, peeled and finely grated

METHOD

Peel half of the oranges so you are left with thin pieces of peel. Julienne the peel and reserve to one side.

Squeeze the oranges into a measuring jug; remove all the pulp and pips but reserve them.

Pour the juice into a large bowl. Make the juice from the oranges up to 3.4 l with cold water.

Place the pulp and pips on a sheet of muslin and tie up into a bag using kitchen twine or string.

Place in the orange liquid, then cover the bowl and leave it overnight.

The next day, pour the liquid and the bag into a saucepan and cook over a medium heat for 40-45 minutes until the peel is soft.

Preheat the oven to 170°C (150° fan) / 325F / gas 3. Place a couple of saucers in the freezer; they will be needed for testing the marmalade's setting point.

Place the jars with their lids in the oven for 10 minutes, to sterilise.

Remove the muslin bag and keep to one side.

Add the sugar to the saucepan and stir well, then squeeze all the liquid contents from the muslin bag back into the saucepan.

Boil the marmalade for 15 minutes, and then remove the saucepan from the heat and spoon a teaspoon of the hot marmalade onto the cold saucers from the freezer; when the marmalade has cooled, prod it to see if a skin has formed. If so, it is ready. If not, continue boiling for 3-4 minutes before testing again.

When ready, remove the pan from the heat and set it to one side.

Fill the sterilised jars with the hot marmalade and seal immediately.

Let the marmalade cool to room temperature before serving.

Makes: four 500 g jars | Preparation time : 15-20 minutes | Cooking time : 1 hour 10 minutes

Orange Marmalade

INGREDIENTS

10 large Seville oranges
750 g / 1 lbs 10 ½ oz / 3 cups granulated sugar
55 g / 2 oz / ¼ cup honey

METHOD

Cut two oranges into discs and set to one side.

Squeeze the remaining oranges into a measuring jug; remove all the pulp and pips but reserve them. Pour the juice into a large bowl.

Make the juice from the oranges up to 3.4 litres with cold water.

Place the pulp and pips on a sheet of muslin and tie up into a bag using kitchen string.

Place in the liquid, then cover the bowl and leave it overnight.

The next day, pour the liquid and the muslin bag into a large saucepan and cook over a medium heat for 40-45 minutes until the peel is soft.

Preheat the oven to 170°C (150°C fan) / 325F / gas 3. Place a couple of saucers in the freezer; they will be needed for testing the setting point.

Place the jars with their lids in the oven to sterilise, for 10 minutes.

Remove the muslin bag and keep to one side until cool enough to handle.

Add the sugar and honey to the saucepan and stir well, then squeeze all the liquid contents from the muslin bag into the saucepan.

Boil the marmalade for 15 minutes, and then remove the saucepan from the heat and spoon a teaspoon of the hot marmalade onto one of the cold saucers from the freezer. When the marmalade has cooled, prod it to see if a skin has formed. If so, it is ready. If not, continue boiling for 3-4 minutes before testing again.

When ready, remove the pan from the heat and set it to one side.

Fill the jars with the hot marmalade and seal immediately.

Let the jars cool to room temperature before serving.

Makes: four 500 g jars | Preparation time : 15-20 minutes | Cooking time : 1 hour 15-20 minutes

Lavender Marmalade

INGREDIENTS

10 large Seville oranges
750 g / 1 lbs 10 ½ oz / 3 cups
granulated sugar
4 small sprigs of fresh lavender

METHOD

Cut and squeeze the oranges into a measuring jug; remove all the pulp and pips but reserve them. Chop the skin and pith into strips.

Pour the juice and chopped peel into a large bowl and stir through the lavender essence.

Make the juice from the oranges and lemons up to 3.4 litres with cold water.

Place the pulp and pips on a sheet of muslin and tie up into a bag using string.

Place in the orange liquid, then cover the bowl and leave it overnight.

The next day, pour the liquid and the muslin bag into a large saucepan and cook over a medium heat for 40-45 minutes until the peel is soft.

Preheat the oven to 170°C (150°C fan) / 325F / gas 3.

Place a couple of saucers in the freezer; they will be needed for testing the marmalade's setting point.

Place the jars with their lids in the oven for 10 minutes to sterilise.

Remove the muslin bag and keep to one side.

Add the sugar and honey to the saucepan and stir well, then squeeze all the liquid contents from the muslin bag back into the saucepan.

Boil the marmalade for 15 minutes, and then remove from the heat and spoon a teaspoon of it onto the cold saucers from the freezer. When the it has cooled, prod it to see if a skin has formed. If so, it is ready. If not, continue boiling for 3-4 minutes before testing again.

When ready, remove the pan from the heat and set it to one side.

Fill the jars with the hot marmalade and place a sprig of lavender in each before sealing immediately.

Let the marmalade cool to room temperature before serving.

Makes: **four 500 g jars** | Preparation time : **15-20 minutes** | Cooking time : **1 hour 10-15 minutes**

Pickles

Pickled Mushrooms

INGREDIENTS

450 g / 1 lb / 6 cups button mushrooms, halved
450 g / 1 lb / 6 cups chestnut mushrooms
110 g / 4 oz / 1 ½ cups shiitake mushrooms, sliced
900 ml / 1 pint 12 fl. oz / 3 ⅗ cups distilled white vinegar
110 g / 4 oz / ½ cup caster (superfine) sugar
4-5 bay leaves
1 tbsp black peppercorns
1 tbsp pickling salt

METHOD

Preheat the oven to 170°C (150° fan) / 325F / gas 3.

Place a large pickling jar in the oven with the lid to sterilise for 10 minutes.

Dissolve the pickling salt and sugar in the vinegar, and then simmer for 5 minutes in a large stainless steel saucepan with the bay leaves and black peppercorns.

Remove the pan from the heat and add all the mushrooms, stirring well.

Remove the pickling jar and lid from the oven.

Ladle the mushrooms and liquid into the jar.

Seal well with the lid, then cover with cheesecloth or dense muslin and tie with string to secure.

Let it cool to room temperature before serving.

Makes: one 1 kg jar | Preparation time : 10 minutes | Cooking time : 20 minutes

Aubergine Pickle

INGREDIENTS

55 ml / 2 fl. oz / ¼ cup olive oil
2 onions
1 clove garlic
450 g / 1 lb / 2 cups vine tomatoes, chopped
2 red peppers, de-seeded and diced
1 large aubergine, finely diced
110 g / 4 oz / ½ cup granulated sugar
75 ml / 3 oz / ⅓ cup distilled white wine vinegar
2 tsp red chilli powder
2 tsp paprika
salt and pepper

METHOD

Heat the olive oil in a large stainless steel saucepan over a medium heat until hot.

Sweat together the onion and garlic, stirring frequently, for 6-7 minutes until the onions softens and starts to turn translucent.

Add the chilli powder and paprika, stir well, and then add the remaining ingredients.

Cover with a lid and cook over a reduced heat for 50-60 minutes until thickened and starting to purée.

As the vegetables are cooking, preheat the oven to 170°C (150° fan) / 325F / gas 3.

Place the jar in the oven with its lid to sterilise it.

Remove after 10 minutes and set it to one side.

Stir the vegetables well and season to taste.

Spoon the mixture into the jar and seal with its lid immediately.

Let it cool to room temperature before serving or storing.

Makes: one 500 g jar | Preparation time : 15 minutes | Cooking time : 1 hour 10 minutes

Pickled Red Cabbage

INGREDIENTS

2 red cabbages, shredded
1.15 l / 2 pints / 4 ⅓ cups distilled white vinegar
30 g / 1 oz / 2 tbsp caster (superfine) sugar
30 g / 1 oz / 2 tbsp salt

METHOD

Place the cabbage in a large bowl and add the sugar and salt.

Toss well, cover and leave overnight.

Strain the cabbage the next day and pat dry.

Preheat the oven to 170°C (150° fan) / 325F / gas 3.

Place the jars with lids in the oven to sterilise.

Remove after 10 minutes and place on a heatproof surface.

Divide the cabbage between the two jars and cover with the vinegar.

Seal and store for 2 weeks before serving.

Makes: **two 500 g jars** | Preparation time : **10-15 minutes** | Cooking time : **10 minutes**

Pickled Carrots

INGREDIENTS

500 g / 1 lbs 2 oz / 3 ⅓ cups carrots,
peeled chopped
750 ml / 1 pint 6 fl. oz / 3 cups red
wine vinegar
3 bay leaves
2 tsp sea salt
1 tsp black peppercorns

METHOD

Preheat the oven to 170°C (150° fan) / 325F / gas 3.

Place the jars in the oven for 10 minutes with their lids, to sterilise.

Meanwhile, combine the vinegar, peppercorns, bay leaves and salt in
a large stainless steel saucepan.

Heat over a medium heat, stirring occasionally to help dissolve the salt.

Once the salt has dissolved into the vinegar, remove the liquid from
the heat and let it cool to one side.

Remove the jars from the oven and place on a heatproof mat.

Spoon the carrots into the jars and pour the un-strained liquid on top
to cover.

Seal well with the lids and let the mixture cool to room temperature.

Pickle the carrots for 1-2 weeks before serving.

Makes: two 500 g jars | Preparation time : 10-15 minutes | Cooking time : 10-15 minutes

Lemon and Sage Anchovies

INGREDIENTS

600 g / 1 lb 5 oz / 3 cups fresh anchovy fillets, pin-boned
900 ml / 1 pint 12 fl. oz / 3 ⅗ cups olive oil
2 lemons
small handful of sage sprigs
salt

METHOD

Lay the anchovy fillets on a flat tray with the flesh side facing up.

Salt well, cover and chill for 2 hours.

Remove the anchovy fillets from the fridge and rinse well under cold running water.

Pat them dry and set to one side.

Preheat the oven to 170°C (150° fan) / 325F / gas 3.

Place the jars in the oven to sterilise for 10 minutes, then remove and place on a heatproof surface.

Peel the zest from the lemons using a vegetable peeler, then cut into thick strips.

Divide the lemon zest between the two jars and add the sage sprigs and anchovy fillets. Cover with the oil.

Seal well and let the jars cool to room temperature.

Store the anchovies in a cool, dry place and let them marinate for 2-3 weeks before using.

Makes: two 500 g jars | Preparation time : 10-15 minutes | Cooking time : 10 minutes

Pickled Garlic

INGREDIENTS

750 ml / 1 pint 6 fl. oz / 3 cups olive oil
2 large bulbs of garlic
2 red chillies
2 orange chillies
2 yellow chillies
2 sprigs rosemary
6 sprigs thyme

METHOD

Preheat the oven to 170°C (150°C fan) / 325F / gas 3.

Place the jars in the oven with their lids to sterilise.

Remove after 10 minutes and place on a heatproof surface or mat.

Use the heel of your palm to crush the garlic bulbs so that the cloves start to separate.

Fill each jar with a bulb of garlic cloves and add the chillies.

Place the rosemary in one jar and the thyme in the other.

Fill with the olive oil before sealing well.

Let the garlic marinade for 2-3 weeks before using for cooking.

Makes: two 500 g jars | Preparation time : 5-10 minutes | Cooking time : 15 minutes

INDEX